Pebble Plus

Hands-On Science Fun

How to Make a
MYSTERY SMELL
BALLOON

Revised Edition

by Lori Shores

Consultant: Ronald Browne, PhD
Department of Elementary & Early Childhood Education
Minnesota State University, Mankato

Download the
Capstone 4D app
for additional content.

 See page 2
for directions.

CAPSTONE PRESS
a capstone imprint

Download the Capstone 4D app!

- Ask an adult to search in the Apple App Store or Google Play for "Capstone 4D".
- Click Install (Android) or Get, then Install (Apple).
- Open the app.
- Scan any of the following spreads with this icon:

When you scan a spread, you'll find fun extra stuff to go with this book!
You can also find these things on the web at www.capstone4D.com
using the password: **balloon.09458**

Pebble Plus is published by Capstone Press,
1710 Roe Crest Drive, North Mankato, Minnesota 56003
www.mycapstone.com

Library of Congress Cataloging-in-Publication Data
is available on the Library of Congress website.

ISBN 978-1-5435-0945-8 (library binding)
ISBN 978-1-5435-0951-9 (paperback)
ISBN 978-1-5435-0957-1 (ebook pdf)

Editorial Credits
Marissa Kirkman, editor; Sarah Bennett, designer;
Tracy Cummins, media researcher; Tori Abraham,
production specialist

Photo Credits
Capstone Studio: Karon Dubke, Cover, 3, 4, 5, 7, 9, 11, 12, 13, 15,
17, 19, 21; Shutterstock: corbac40, Cover Design Element

Note to Parents and Teachers

The Hands-On Science Fun set supports national science
standards related to physical science. This book describes and
illustrates making a mystery smell balloon. The images support
early readers in understanding the text. The repetition of words
and phrases helps early readers learn new words. This book
also introduces early readers to subject-specific vocabulary
words, which are defined in the Glossary section. Early readers
may need assistance to read some words and to use the Table of
Contents, Glossary, Read More, Internet Sites, Critical Thinking
Questions, and Index sections of the book.

Printed and bound in the United States of America.
010772S18

Table of Contents

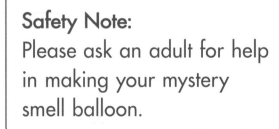

Safety Note:
Please ask an adult for help in making your mystery smell balloon.

Getting Started

What's that smell?

Only you will know that

it's a mystery smell balloon.

Your friends won't believe

their noses!

Here's what you need:

1 latex balloon

fork

1 clove of garlic

ribbon
or string

small funnel

Other smells to try:

1 teaspoon (5 mL) vanilla extract
1 teaspoon (5 mL) pickle juice
crushed onion

Making the Secret Smell

Peel the skin off

the clove of garlic.

Crush the clove with the fork.

The garlic will be squished

and juicy.

Slide the small end of
the funnel in the opening
of the balloon.

Carefully dump the wet garlic
down the funnel.

Next, blow up the balloon
as big as you can.

Tie the end of the balloon
and shake it around.

Sneak into a crowded room.
Tie the balloon to a chair
or doorknob using a ribbon.

Now watch as your friends
notice the smell!

How Does It Work?

Smelly things give off

tiny pieces called molecules.

They are too small to see.

You smell garlic when

the molecules reach your nose.

Garlic molecules

pass through tiny holes

in the balloon.

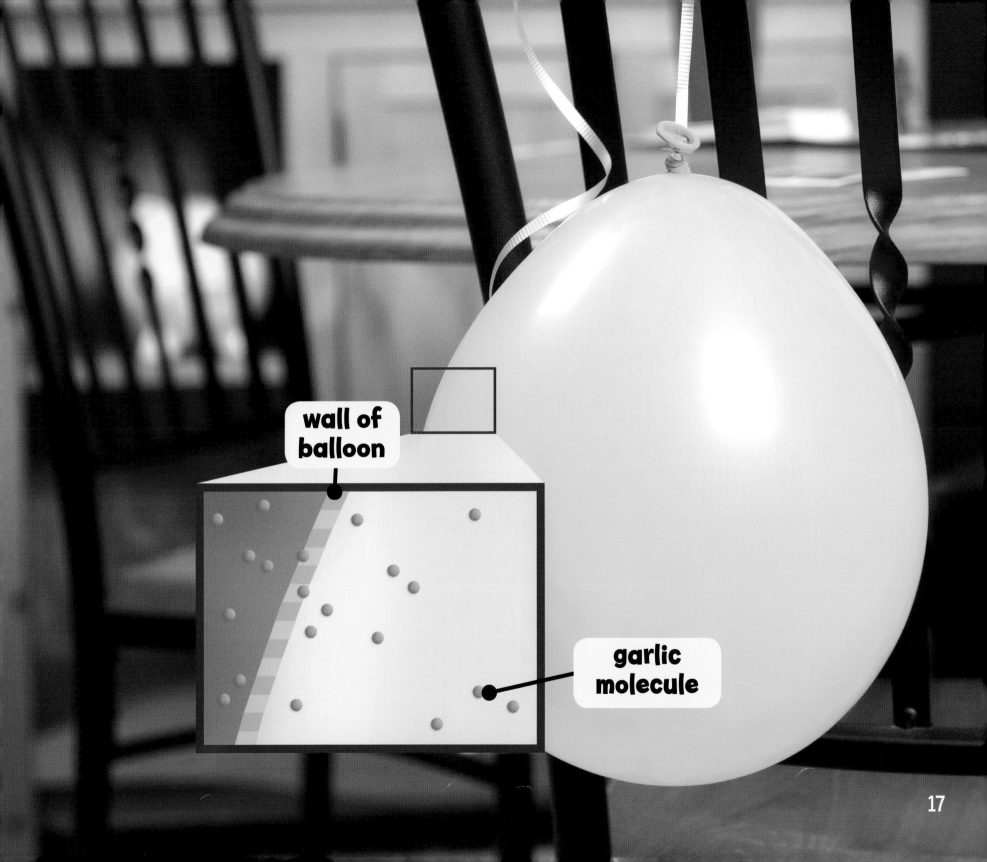

wall of balloon

garlic molecule

Air molecules are bigger.

They can't pass through

the holes as easily.

Air stays in the balloon longer

than the garlic molecules.

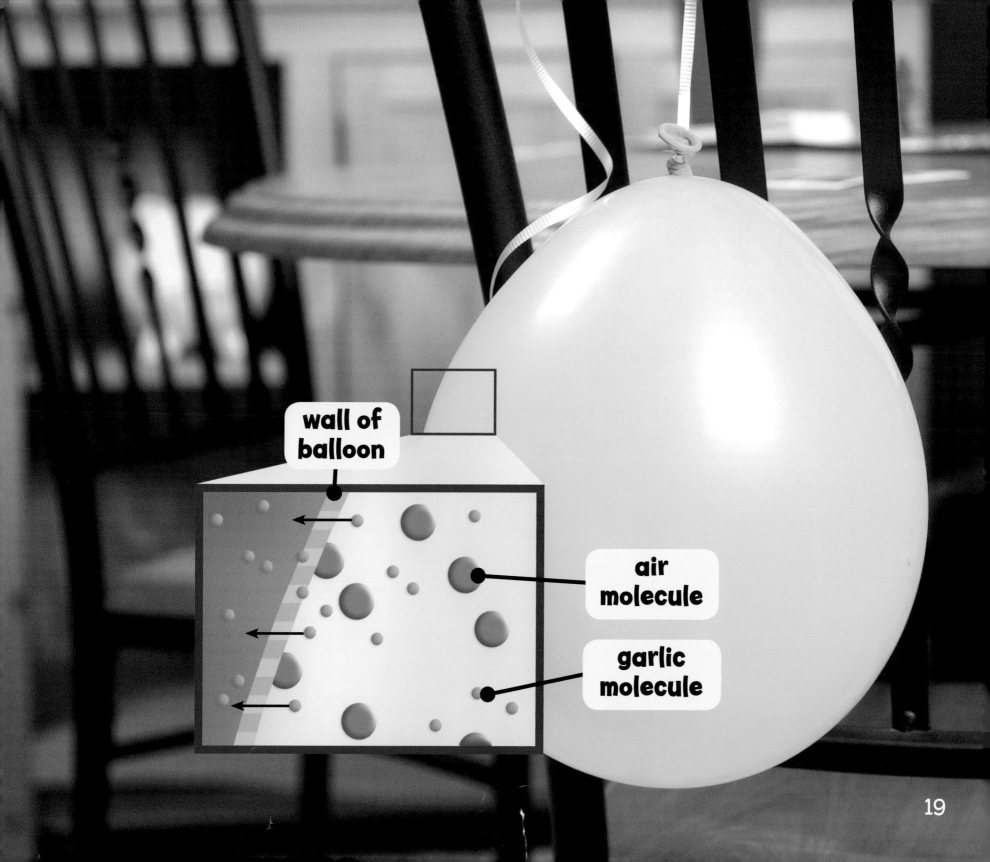

wall of balloon

air molecule

garlic molecule

The tiny garlic molecules
spread through the air.
Your friends crinkle their noses
as they sniff the molecules.

Glossary

clove—one of the sections of a bulb of garlic

crinkle—to wrinkle up

funnel—an open cone that narrows to a tube

molecule—the smallest part of an element that can exist and still keep the characteristics of the element

peel—to remove the outer skin

Read More

Huffman, Julie. *101 Ways to Gross Out Your Friends.* Lake Forest, Calif.: Quarto Publishing Group, 2016.

Miller, Rachel, Holly Homer, and Jamie Harrington. *The 101 Coolest Simple Science Experiments.* Salem, Mass.: Page Street Publishing Co., 2016.

Oyler, Amy. *Pop, Sizzle, Boom!: 101 Science Experiments for the Mad Scientist in Every Kid.* New York: St. Martin's Press, 2017.

Internet Sites

Use FactHound to find Internet sites related to this book.

Visit *www.facthound.com*

Just type **9781543509458** and go.

Super-cool stuff! Check out projects, games and lots more at **www.capstonekids.com**

Critical Thinking Questions

1. How does the secret smell get inside of the balloon?

2. How does the smell get out of the balloon?

3. Describe why air molecules don't pass through the balloon as quickly as other molecules.

Index